SPECIMEN INTERPRETATION PASSAGES
for
REVISED HIGHER ENGLISH

Revised Edition

This revised edition takes account of the amendments to the Arrangements introduced by the Board.

by

Helen J. Davidson

ISBN 0 7169 8007 x
© *H.J. Davidson, 1992.*

The specimen passages and questions printed in this publication reflect the author's opinion of what might be expected in a Revised Higher English examination.

ROBERT GIBSON · Publisher
17 Fitzroy Place, Glasgow, G3 7SF.

INTRODUCTION

This book contains a selection of sample interpretation passages covering as wide a variety of material as possible. Any candidate sitting the Revised Higher English examination who completes these papers should have covered most of the types of questions they could expect to meet in the examination.

Although tackling these test papers is an essential part in preparing for the examination, this preparation can only be achieved in the first instance by candidates developing comprehension and understanding skills through wide reading, general interest and understanding of topical issues.

The first two question papers have answer schemes to indicate the kind of answers one could expect. Obviously they do not cover every possible answer as there is more than one way of giving a correct answer. You are advised to tackle these question papers first and then compare your solutions with the sample solutions at the back of the book.

There is also, at the back of the book, a glossary of terms which will help you in discussions of language and style.

INSTRUCTIONS TO CANDIDATES

Part I — Interpretation

You should spend approximately ONE HOUR and FIVE MINUTES on this part of the paper.

Read the passage (or two passages) and then answer, as far as possible in your own words, the questions which follow.

ADVICE ON
INTERPRETATION
ANSWERS

One Passage

Read the passage carefully once to get a general impression of it. Look at the questions to check which aspects of the passage you are going to be asked about. Read the passage again carefully to check the details. Answer the questions set.

Two Passages

Read both passages once to get a general impression of each.

Read the first passage again more carefully to make sure you understand the details. Answer the questions set. Now re-read the second passage and answer the questions. You should now be ready to compare the two passages. They will certainly have a similarity of subject matter or theme which should by now be clear to you. The difference may lie in the details and in the style. The questions will help you.

The questions will be about

      MEANING: Vocabulary
                      Argument
                      Ideas

      STYLE: Syntax
                      Vocabulary   If you are unsure of any of these terms
                      Imagery   refer to "Glossary" on page 55
                      Tone   before attempting the passages.
                      Register

MEANING

Vocabulary

Wide reading should improve your basic vocabulary. Try in your spare time to read at least one serious newspaper article a week.

Always check unknown words in a dictionary.

Context will help with unfamiliar words. Context is that part of the passage which is close to the word(s) with which you are not familiar.

Look for **clues** from the adjoining text:

        Words linked by *and* etc., which have a **similar** meaning;
        Words preceded by *not* etc., which have the **opposite** meaning;
        Explanations coming before or after the word;
        Examples which clarify the meaning.

Argument

Read carefully.

Note the number of marks: a mark usually indicates the amount of detail required, e.g., 2 marks indicate **two** reasons being asked for;
4 marks indicate each reason requires further explanation.

Use your **common sense**; trace the argument carefully.

Make sure you do not skip a stage in the argument.

Look carefully at conjunctions (because, if, etc.) which will guide you on the connections between ideas.

Use your **general knowledge** to assist you.

Consider the **wider context** which may help you, **but** make sure you discuss only the arguments put forward in the passage. **Do not** present your own arguments unless **clearly** asked to.

Use your own words to indicate that you have understood.

Sometimes you are asked to provide an example from **your own knowledge** to illustrate a general idea raised in the passage. Here you do give an example from your own experience not one from the passage.

You might be asked to explain the inclusion of an **anecdote** in a passage. It will usually be an **example** to **illustrate** the argument being put forward.

Paragraphs should now be clear to you.
You should note the topic of each.
You might be asked about the **opening** sentence.
This may introduce a new aspect of the passage's main topic.
The **closing** sentence may sum up.

A very common question is about the links between paragraphs. The first or last sentence may contain one reference to the previous paragraph; one to the following paragraph. You will be expected to comment on this.

The **title** of a passage usually sums up the theme.
It anticipates what is to come.
The **style** will often be significant, e.g., Alliteration to catch the interest; a Question to which the passage will give an answer.

The **final sentence** usually sums up an article.
It may try to provoke further discussion, e.g., a question.
It may give a final example.

The **overall structure** will now be clear.
The general idea or **theme** should be clear.

The **purpose** should be clear.
Decide whether the writer is writing in order to explain, attack, mock, observe, etc. his subject.

If you have been given two passages you will find that when you have studied both passages in similar detail you will be able to compare their ideas, arguments and style.

STYLE

You will also be expected to comment on why the writer has presented what he has to say in a particular way. Does his style help him to present his ideas? You will have discussed style often in school. You must now use all the knowledge you have gathered. Remember: merely to notice that a particular technical device has been used is not enough; you must say **why** it has been used and whether **you** think it has been used **effectively**.

Technical terms may be useful but they are not essential. If you can express what you have observed without them, do so, but you may find them helpful.

QUESTION PAPER A

Refer to page 2 for Instructions to Candidates

The first passage is taken from an essay by Laurie Lee entitled *Writing Autobiography*. The second passage is adapted from the introduction to *My Experiment with Truth* by Mahatma Gandhi.

PASSAGE 1

Autobiography can be the laying to rest of ghosts as well as an ordering of the mind. But for me it is also a celebration of living and an attempt to hoard its sensations.

In common with other writers I have written little that was not for the most part
5   autobiographical. The spur for me is the fear of evaporation — erosion, amnesia, if you like — the fear that a whole decade may drift gently away and leave nothing but a salt-caked mud-flat.

A wasting memory is not only a destroyer; it can deny one's very existence. A day unremembered is like a soul unborn, worse than if it had never been. What
10   indeed was that summer if it is not recalled? That journey? That act of love? To whom did it happen if it has left you with nothing? Certainly not to you. So any bits of warm life preserved by the pen are trophies snatched from the dark, are branches of leaves fished out of the flood, are tiny arrests of mortality.

The urge to write may also be the fear of death — particularly with
15   autobiography — the need to leave messages for those who come after, saying, "I was here; I saw it too". Then there are the other uses of autobiography, some less poignant than these assurances — exposure, confession, apologia, revenge, or even staking one's claim to a godhead. In writing my first volume of autobiography, *Cider with Rosie* (1959), I was moved by several of these needs,
20   but the chief one was celebration: to praise the life I'd had and so preserve it, and to live again both the good and the bad . . .

There is, however, the question of truth, of fact, often raised about autobiography. If dates are wrong, can the book still be true? If facts err, can feelings be false? One would prefer to have truth both in fact and feeling (if
25   either could ever be proved). And yet . . . I remember recording some opinions held by my mother which she had announced during a family wedding. "You got your mother all wrong," complained an aunt. "That wasn't at Edie's wedding, it was Ethel's."

Ours is a period of writing particularly devoted to facts, to a fondness for data
30   rather than divination, as though to possess the exact measurements of the Taj Mahal is somehow to possess its spirit. I read in a magazine recently a profile of

6

Chicago whose every line was a froth of statistics. It gave me a vivid picture, not so much of the city, but of the author cramped in the archives.

In writing autobiography, especially one that looks back at childhood, the only
35 truth is what you remember. No one else who was there can agree with you because he has his own version of what he saw. He also holds to a personal truth of himself, based on indefatigable self-regard. One neighbour's reaction, after reading my book, sums up this double vision: "You hit off old Tom to the life," he said. "But why d'you tell all those lies about me?"

40 Seven brothers and sisters shared my early years, and we lived on top of each other. If they all had written of those days, each account would have been different, and each one true. We saw the same events at different heights, at different levels of mood and hunger — one suppressing an incident as too much to bear, another building it large around him, each reflecting one world
45 according to the temper of his day, his age, the chance heat of his blood. Recalling it differently, as we were bound to do, what was it, in fact, we saw? Which one among us has the truth of it now? And which one shall be the judge? The truth is, of course, that there is no pure truth, only the moody accounts of witnesses.

PASSAGE 2

It is not my purpose to attempt a real autobiography. I simply want to tell the story of my numerous experiments with truth and as my life consists of nothing but these experiments, it is true that the story will take the shape of an autobiography. I should certainly like to narrate my experiments in the spiritual
5 field which are known only to myself, and from which I have derived such power as I possess for working in the political field. If the experiments are really spiritual, then there can be no room for self-praise. They can only add to my humility. The more I reflect and look back on the past, the more vividly do I feel my limitations.

10 What I want to achieve — what I have been striving and pining to achieve these thirty years — is self-realisation, to see God face to face, to attain *moksha**. I live and move and have my being in pursuit of this goal. All that I do by way of speaking and writing, and all my ventures in the political field, are directed to this same end. But as I have all along believed that what is possible for one is
15 possible for all, my experiments have not been conducted in the closet, but in the open: and I do not think that this fact detracts from their spiritual value. There are some things which are known only to oneself and one's Maker. These are clearly incommunicable. The experiments I am about to relate are not such. But they are spiritual, or rather moral; for the essence of religion is morality.

* Literally freedom from birth and death. The nearest English equivalent is 'Salvation'.

20 Only those matters of religion that can be comprehended as much by children as
    by older people will be included in this story. If I can narrate them in a
    dispassionate and humble spirit, many other experiments will find in them
    provision for their onward march. Far be it from me to claim any degree of
    perfection for these experiments. I claim for them nothing more than does a
25 scientist who, though he conducts his experiments with the utmost accuracy,
    forethought and minuteness, never claims any finality about his conclusions, but
    keeps an open mind regarding them. I have gone through deep self-introspection,
    searched myself through and through, and examined and analysed every
    psychological situation. Yet I am far from claiming any finality or infallibility
30 about my conclusions. One claim I do indeed make and it is this. For me they
    appear to be absolutely correct, and seem for the time being to be final. For if
    they were not, I should base no action on them. But at every step I have carried
    out the process of acceptance or rejection and acted accordingly. And so long as
    my acts satisfy my reason and my heart, I must firmly adhere to my original
35 conclusions.

Questions on Passage 1

Marks

(a) Show how the immediate context of 'arrests of mortality' (line 13) helps
you to arrive at its meaning.   **2**

(b) '. . . exposure, confession, apologia, revenge, or even staking one's claim
to a godhead.' (lines 17 – 18)
In what circumstances might an author writing his autobiography use any
one of the above?   **2**

(c) Explain; '. . . one suppressing an incident as too much to bear, another
building it large around him . . .' (lines 43 – 44).
(Your explanation, if you wish, may take the form of an example, perhaps
from your own experience, of such a situation.)   **2**

(d) Read carefully the first paragraph of the passage (lines 1 – 3).

   (i) Of all the reasons Laurie Lee gives for writing autobiography, which
   for him are the more personal? You should try in your answer to use
   your own words.   **2**

   (ii) By what means does he indicate in the paragraph that these are the
   more personal reasons?   **1**

(e) 'A wasting memory is not only a destroyer; it can also deny one's very
existence.' (line 8)
Show that this sentence relates to what has gone before and at the same time
introduces the idea to be developed in the remainder of the paragraph.   **4**

8

(f) What is the significance of the anecdote (lines 25 – 28) in illustrating the author's argument in paragraphs 5 and 6 (lines 22 – 33)? **2**

(g) '. . . may <u>drift</u> gently away and leave nothing behind but a <u>salt-caked mud-flat</u>.' (lines 6 – 7)
By considering carefully the word choice, particularly those underlined, comment on the effectiveness of the image. **3**

(18)

Questions on Passage 2

(h) Gandhi does not claim that he is writing an autobiography.
Explain in your own words his reason for telling the story of his life. **2**

(i) '. . . my experiments have not been conducted in the closet,' (line 15).
Comment on the effectiveness of this image and explain how it relates to his argument in the rest of paragraph 2. **4**

(j) Gandhi compares himself to a scientist. How does he justify the comparison? **4**

(k) 'infallibility' (line 29).
How does the context help you to understand the meaning of this word? **2**

(12)

Questions on Both Passages

(l) (i) '. . . there is no pure truth, only the moody accounts of witnesses.' (lines 48 – 49)
Explain what you think Laurie Lee means by this. **2**
 (ii) 'self-realisation' (line 11).
Using the note to help you, explain what you think Gandhi meant by this. **2**

(m) From your reading of the first passage say what kind of person you think Laurie Lee must be.
Give one piece of evidence from the passage to explain it. **3**

(n) From your reading of the second passage say what kind of person you think Gandhi was.
Give one piece of evidence from the passage and explain it. **3**

(10)

Total marks (40)

Compare your answers with the answers given on pages 43 – 48

QUESTION PAPER B

Refer to page 2 for Instructions to Candidates

The first passage is an extract from an article in *SHE* magazine by Judith Cook. The second is an extract from the fantasy novel *The Wounded Land* by Stephen Donaldson.

PASSAGE 1

> *A hole the size of America has appeared in the Earth's protective layer. If the
> ozone sun-shield continues to break up we will all be in danger.*
> Judith Cook reports.

Early one wet cold morning years ago I rushed out of the hotel in which I was
staying, leapt in the car to get to an assignment for my newspaper and — it
wouldn't start. I tried helplessly to get it to go and finally had to ring the AA. The
man "who does know" arrived an hour or so later, opened the bonnet, wiped
5 the plugs and their leads and gave them a quick spray from an aerosol can.
Magic! It started straight away. Since when I have never gone anywhere without
a can of the magic substance more or less chained to the boot.

That kind of thing has happened to all of us. Aerosol sprays are something we
just never think about. We go to the hairdresser's and spend two hours and lots
10 of money on (in my case) possibly unmanageable hair and outside the wind howls
and the rain pours. "Give it a good spray, shall I madam?" "Oh yes, please do."

You have a dirty oven? Just spray on *Smashgrease*, wait five minutes and wipe it
off. The cat has a few friends in overnight? So give the carpet a few good squirts
of shampoo from the handy can.

15 Last year nearly 700 million aerosol cans were produced in Britain and about one
third of those used "chlorofluorocarbons" or "CFCs" as a propellant.

**OZONE (O_3) is an explosive, highly toxic, pale blue gas which occurs naturally in
the earth's stratosphere in small amounts about 15 – 30 miles above the earth's
surface. It absorbs solar ultraviolet radiation which otherwise could cause severe
20 damage to organisms on earth. It is thought that life on land was only possible
when the ozone layer was formed some 425 000 000 years ago. Without our
protective shield we'd be dead from radiation in about one hour.**

CFCs are the group of chemicals which are used as propellants in aerosols, in the
manufacture of polystyrene foams and in the circulation systems of refrigerators.
25 CFCs are used to produce disposable cartons in which we put products like

10

takeaway hamburgers. When the containers are squashed up and thrown away, CFCs get into the atmosphere just like those in sprays.

So what? For a long time nobody gave this convenient way of dispensing products
a second thought. Then, in 1974, suggestions began to circulate in scientific
30   circles that something was going badly wrong with the Ozone layer. Ozone is a
gas made up of three oxygen molecules and varies considerably in thickness. It is
at its densest between 10 and 30 km above the surface of the earth. It is not,
according to the experts, present in huge amounts and if all the ozone molecules
in the stratosphere were gathered together they would form a layer no thicker
35   than a one pound coin.

But this seemingly thin and unimportant layer of gases soaks up ultra-violet rays
and stops potentially lethal levels of radiation reaching the earth. Gradually it
became apparent that a large hole was appearing in the Ozone layer over
America between September and November every year. It has assumed gigantic
40   proportions — the size of the United States of America and as deep as Mount
Everest is high. Scientists who began to blame CFCs for the hole received short
shrift — at first. Now few would argue that CFCs are not a major cause of it.

The most obvious worry is that the Ozone layer filters out the ultraviolet rays
which can cause skin cancer. The environment lobby, including Friends of the
45   Earth, argue that the most likely effect of a large hole in the layer is a skin cancer
epidemic. Other nasty effects would include eye diseases such as cataracts, severe
damage to agricultural crops, a worsening of pollution in cities like London,
Athens and Los Angeles and even dramatic and irreversible changes in weather
patterns as man-made chemicals interact with natural ones.

PASSAGE 2

Early in the dawn, Sunder roused Covenant and Linden so that they would have
time to break their fast before the sun rose. Sunder was tense and distracted,
anticipating a change in the Sunbane. When they had eaten, they went down to
the river bank and found a stretch of flat rock where they could stand to await
5   the morning. Through the gaunt and blackened trees, they saw the sun cast its
first glance over the horizon.

It appeared baleful, fiery and red; it wore coquelicot like a crown of thorns, and
cast a humid heat entirely unlike the fierce intensity of the desert sun. Its corona
seemed insidious and detrimental. Linden's eyes flinched at the sight. And
10   Sunder's face was strangely blanched. He made an instinctive warding gesture
with both hands. "Sun of pestilence," he breathed and his tone winced. "Ah, we
have been fortunate. Had this sun come upon us after the desert sun, or the
fertile —" The thought died in his throat.

"How so?" asked Covenant. He did not understand the attitude of his companions. "What does this sun do?"

15   "Do?" Sunder gritted. "What harm does it not? It is the dread and torment of the Land. Still water becomes stagnant. Growing things rot and crumble. All who eat or drink of that which has not been shaded are afflicted with a disease which few survive and none can cure. And the insects —!"

"He's right," whispered Linden with her mouth full of dismay. "Oh, my God!"

20   "It is the Mithil river which makes us fortunate, for it will not stagnate. Until another desert sun, it will continue to flow from its springs, and from the rain. And it will warn us in other ways also." The reflected red in Sunder's eyes made him look like a cornered animal. "Yet I cannot behold such a sun without faint-heartedness. My people hide in their homes at such a time. I ache to be hidden
25   also. I am homeless and small against the wideness of the world, and in all the Land I fear a sun of pestilence more than any other thing."

Sunder's frank apprehension affected Covenant like guilt. To answer it, he said, "You're also the only reason we're still alive."

"Yes," Sunder responded as if he were listening to his own thoughts rather than
30   to Covenant.

"Yes!" Covenant snapped. "And some day everyone is going to know that this Sunbane is not the only way to live. When that day comes, you're going to be just about the only person in the Land who can teach them anything.

Sunder was silent for a time. Then he asked distantly, "What will I teach them?"

35   "To re-make the Land." Deliberately, Covenant included Linden in his passion. "It used to be a place of such health and loveliness — if you saw it, it would break your heart." His voice gave off gleams of rage and love. "That can be true again." He glared at his companions, daring them to doubt him.

Linden covered her gaze, but Sunder turned and met Covenant's ire. "Your
40   words have no meaning. No man or woman can re-make the Land. It is in the hands of the Sunbane, for good or ill. Yet this I say to you," he grated as Covenant began to protest. "Make the attempt." Retrieving his sack, he went brusquely and tied it to the centre of the raft.

"I hear you," Covenant muttered. He felt an unexpected desire for violence.
45   "I hear you."

12

Questions on Passage 1

Marks

(a) In what way does the opening paragraph (lines 1 – 7) contribute to the author's argument? **3**

(b) The author is making two further points about our attitude to aerosols in Paragraph 2 (lines 8 – 11). Explain what these points are. **2**

(c) The paragraph about Ozone (lines 17 – 22) is clearly separate from its context, as there are no linking words and the print is different.

   (i) What in your opinion is the effect of placing it in this position in the text and having it printed in this way? **2**

   (ii) Quote a sentence from later in the passage which makes clear that this paragraph is nonetheless a part of the discussion about aerosols. **1**

(d) "potentially" (line 37). How does the context help you to arrive at the meaning of this word? **2**

(e) Explain the use of inverted commas in line 4 — "who does know". **1**

(f) Examine carefully lines 12 – 14. By commenting on the sentence structure and word choice show how the style adds to the impact of this paragraph on the author's argument. **4**

(g) "no thicker than a one pound coin". Comment on the effectiveness of this image. **2**

(h) (i) Explain in your own words the main function of the Ozone layer. **1**

   (ii) Which of the effects of the hole in the Ozone layer does the author appear to think will interest the average magazine reader? Explain your choice. **2**

(20)

Questions on Passage 2

(i) ". . . like a crown of thorns,"
Discuss the significance of this image in line 7. **2**

(j) What are the consequences of a "sun of pestilence"? **2**

(k) What, according to Sunder, is the advantage and what is the disadvantage of their present position? **2**

(l) This is an extract from a series of novels. What clue is there that Covenant has been to this place before? **1**

13

(m) Why do you think he uses the expression "re-make" (line 35) and why has
Land got a capital letter?   **2**

(n) ". . . his tone winced." (line 11)
OR
". . . her mouth full of dismay." (line 19)
Comment on the effectiveness of **one** of these expressions.   **1**
     (10)

Questions on Both Passages

(o) Which of the changes scientifically predicted in the first passage appears to
have actually happened in the second passage?   **2**

(p) Both passages are about pollution but one is from a magazine and the other
is from a fantasy novel.
  (i) Look at lines 32 – 41 of the first passage. How does the writer arouse
our fears?   **2**
  (ii) Look at the lines 35 – 38 of the second passage. How does the writer
arouse an emotional response here?   **2**

(q) Consider the style of each passage and explain how you would have known
immediately that one was from a magazine and one from a novel.   **4**
     (10)
     Total marks (40)

Compare your answers with the sample answers given on pages 49 – 54

QUESTION PAPER C

Refer to page 2 for Instructions to Candidates

The first passage is an extract from *Healey's Eye* by Dennis Healey, and the second is an extract from an article in the *New Internationalist* by Peter Stalker.

PASSAGE 1

Since its earliest days people have worried about the status of photography. Is it art or reality? To begin with, a photograph has a direct physical relationship with its subject which none of the arts can claim. The negative is made by light reflected from the subject itself; when Europeans first took their cameras to
5 China a century ago, the Mandarins they photographed saw their portraits as a physical emanation of themselves. The photographer can doctor his negative in various ways when he is developing or printing it; but essentially his job is to choose his position, his lighting and the decisive moment for pressing the button. Then he lets the light make the picture — he only takes the photograph.

10 A painter on the other hand actually makes the picture himself. However faithfully he aims to represent his subject, he has to choose his medium, mix and lay on the colours; in deciding how to do so he will be influenced by what he knows and feels about the subject as well as what he sees. He must confront his subject for hours, days and even years, learning as he looks and paints, and
15 thinking all the time about what it means to him. Compared with a painting, every photograph is a snapshot even if the shutter is open for a few minutes rather than 1/100 second.

Then is a photograph more realistic than a painting? Contrary to the old saying, the camera can lie as easily as the paint brush — and more effectively,
20 because so many people believe it reproduces reality. It does not. It reproduces appearance, which as we all know, is quite a different thing. Philosophers have argued for centuries about the relationship between appearance and reality. Ordinary people know that the appearance of a person depends on all sorts of factors which have nothing to do with reality at all — the mood of the person at
25 the time, clothes, make-up, lighting, position and so on. A photograph does not even represent the appearance of an object to the human being who sees it; it reproduces a mechanical image of the object at one fraction of a second out of millions which might have been chosen, from one particular viewpoint out of hundreds, and in one particular light. It takes a three-dimensional object which
30 exists in time, freezes it and flattens it out on a piece of paper.

But even when we know that the photographer has done his work of selection so as to produce the particular effect he wants, we also know that the image itself is a mechanical reproduction of what the image really was in that split-second. That

is why old photographs have such a fascination for us. As Susan Sontag says, if
35 we could choose between an authentic painting of Shakespeare and a
contemporary photograph, most of us would choose the photograph because in
this sense at least it is more "real". So perhaps the African tribesmen who turned
their faces away from my camera and the Arabs who chased me through the
Soukh in Damascus were not entirely wrong in seeing a photograph as capturing
40 something of themselves which no one else should have. There is an element of
theft in taking a picture — and of aggression too. It is no accident that people talk
of shooting pictures.

Once you are bitten by the camera bug there is a real danger of preferring the
photograph to reality and of seeing everything as an object to be shot. A tourist
45 was describing a beggar he had seen in Cairo, blind, without arms or legs, and
covered with flies. "What did you give him?" asked a friend. "A hundredth of a
second at f11," was the reply. I do not think my wife has ever quite forgiven me
for taking a photograph of the doctor's jeep arriving when she had broken her
ankle while we were camping in the Alps.

PASSAGE 2

The photo on the front of this month's *New Internationalist* makes me uneasy.
The Indian man is pleasant looking, certainly not aggressive and what he is
holding is only a camera.

Yet there is a threat, for he is about to take my photograph — a hostile act if the
5 language of photography is anything to go by. His camera is 'loaded' with film.
Lenses are attached with a 'bayonet' mechanism. And now he is about to take
some 'shots' and 'capture' my image on film.

I'm not sure I want to be shot, or even captured, in this way. For a start I have no
idea who this person is. What right does he have to take my picture? What right
10 does he have to use a camera at all? The instrument looks entirely out of place in
his hands. This photograph raises for me a whole series of tricky issues —
technical, social and racial — that I find difficult to resolve.

You'd think we'd no longer be sensitive to such things. Human beings have
been photographing each other for the last 150 years. Snapshots are a
15 commonplace of daily life; around two billion are taken each year. And the mass
media are filled with photographic images which we absorb without a second
thought — usually without even a first one.

On the other hand there are people who spend their working lives thinking about
such things — who take the time to analyze just what photographs mean and how
20 we react to them. Photography is indeed a happy hunting ground for

16

communication theorists. And there is a whole abstract science of 'semiology' with which you can confuse yourself if you are so inclined.

If you are not, the safest and most solid ground on which to start is with the camera itself. You can consider it as just a piece of technology: another tool
25 which offers us greater control over the world. Fleeting moments can be snatched from the confusion and chaos all around to be enjoyed and admired at leisure. Cameras have become so simple and relatively cheap to use that this freezing of time is a very democratic option available to almost all consumers in Western countries.

30 But as with all such technology there is a hidden cost: while intensifying one human experience they can simultaneously displace others . . . Jet aircraft, for example, whisk us around the world in a matter of hours but cut us off from experience of progressive travel. Recorded music offers endless listening pleasure but excludes the spontaneity of live performance. And photography too
35 intensifies our vision of certain aspects of our lives while excluding others from the viewfinder.

This is evident even in the family photo album. Everyone smiles their way through birthday parties, marriages, holidays and Christmas presents. But pleasant as such snapshots might be, they offer a slanted and partial view of our
40 lives. There are few images of argument or fights. There are no battered babies on the sheepskin rugs. Divorces and funerals go unrecorded. The technology of photography permits, and requires, selectivity. And the conventional selection amplifies nostalgia and keeps a record of life which relegates unpleasantness to the uncertainty and dimness of memory.

Questions on Passage 1

Marks

(a) From your reading of paragraphs 1 and 2 (lines 1 – 17) what are the **two** important points that the author makes about a photographer taking a picture, and what **two** important points does he make about a painter making a picture?

4

(b) "Contrary to the old saying, the camera can lie as easily as a paint brush — and more effectively . . ." (lines 18 – 19).

   (i) What distinction is suggested in the paragraph between appearance and reality?

2

   (ii) What further point does Healey make about the way in which a photograph represents appearance?

2

(c) Show in what way the writer's reference to the Arabs in Damascus (lines 38 – 41) contributes to his argument.   2

(d) Healey also claims that there is an element of aggression in taking photographs. From your own knowledge can you think of a suitable example of photographic aggression.   2

(e) Examine carefully the sentence "A photograph does not . . . light" (lines 25 – 29). By COMMENTING on structure and word-choice, indicate how EFFECTIVE you consider this sentence to be.   4

(16)

Questions on Passage 2

(f) How does the writer prove that the language of photography is hostile? Give at least **four** examples of the point he is making. Indicate one at least that has been mentioned in Dennis Healey's article.   4

(g) What danger does he see in the way we look at photographs in the media?   2

(h) (i) Look at lines 23 – 29.
Explain what Peter Stalker sees as the one great advantage of photography.   2

(ii) Look at lines 34 – 44.
Explain what he sees as the disadvantages of photography.   4

(12)

Questions on Both Passages

(i) Both writers discuss photography. By close reference to the passages show in what position each of them sees himself in relation to the camera, at least at one point during his discussion.   2

(j) Quote and explain an expression linked to time which occurs in both passages.   2

(k) Though there are some resemblances in style, on the whole the passages are very different. Point out at least **two** language features from EACH PASSAGE and explain which passage you prefer.   8

(12)

Total marks (40)

18

QUESTION PAPER D

Refer to page 2 for Instructions to Candidates

The first passage is an extract from *The Heyday of Natural History* by Lynn Barber in which she considers some of the reasons for the popularity of the study of nature during the Victorian era. The second is a group of extracts from the autobiography and journals of Charles Darwin, author of *The Origin of the Species*.

PASSAGE 1

Every Victorian young lady, it seemed could reel off the names of twenty different kinds of fern or fungus, and every Victorian clergyman nurtured a secret ambition to publish a natural history of his parish in imitation of Gilbert White. By the middle of the century, there was hardly a middle-class drawing-room in
5 the country that did not contain an aquarium, a fern-case, a butterfly cabinet, a seaweed album, a shell collection, or some other evidence of a taste for natural history, and at the same period it was impossible to visit the seaside without tripping over parties of earnest ladies and gentlemen, armed with a book by Mr. Gosse and a collection of jamjars, standing knee-deep in rock-pools and
10 prodding at sea-anemones. Every newspaper ran a natural history section, and every correspondence column became a periodic battleground for debates about whether swallows could hibernate, or whether toads could live for centuries immured in blocks of stone. Natural history was a national obsession, and books on the subject were only marginally less popular than the works of Dickens.
15 One quite undistinguished natural history book, *Common Objects of the Country* by the Rev. J.G. Wood, sold 100,000 copies in a week.

Victorian naturalists rejoiced in their new-found popularity, but they were also secretly rather puzzled by it. Those who tried to account for it came up with conflicting and often insubstantial explanations. One American writer, for
20 instance, claimed that it was all thanks to two inventions, the aquarium and the microscope; but since the aquarium was not invented until 1850, by which time the tide of natural history was running at full flood, and the microscope had been invented two centuries earlier, this explanation is unconvincing. Several writers tried to argue that the reason for natural history's popularity was that there were
25 so many great naturalists alive and so many important new discoveries being made every year. But this again is implausible, since the period of natural history's greatest popularity coincided with a period of singular stagnation in biological progress. In fact it seems more likely that it was lack of serious scientific advance that made the popular addiction to natural history possible,
30 since it is always easier for the layman to follow a subject when it is not undergoing any revolutions.

Perhaps part of the charm of natural history, to the Victorians, was that it was not studied at school. Schools not only ignored scientific subjects, but positively discouraged them. Darwin was reprimanded by his headmaster at Shrewsbury for
35 "wasting his time" on experiments. In consequence, those adults who did take up the study of natural history came to it with all the freshness of unalloyed ignorance. Queen Victoria learned only in middle age that kangaroos carried their young in pouches, and some of her courtiers were quite astounded by the news that tadpoles turned into frogs. The microscope was not then the loathed
40 and dreaded piece of schoolroom equipment that it is today: on the contrary, an "evening at the microscope" was a fashionable after-dinner entertainment.

Evenings at the microscope, visits to the new zoological gardens and public aquaria, forays into the rock-pools, and magic lantern lectures on the Life History of the Bee all came under the heading "rational amusement", and
45 there was nothing that well-to-do Victorians sought for so avidly as that in order to fill their seemingly interminable leisure hours. To qualify as rational amusement — as distinct from vulgar or 'mere' amusement, like going to the theatre or reading novels — an activity had to contain some element of useful instruction or moral uplift; preferably both. Natural history fitted the bill
50 perfectly. It was scientific, and there was nothing more useful than science, as everybody knew. It was morally uplifting, because it enabled one to find "sermons in stone, and good in everything". It was healthy, since it involved going out of doors. For gentlemen it offered new pretexts to go out and shoot something, and for ladies it offered new subjects for water-colours, for albums,
55 or for embroidery. It also tied in very conveniently with the contemporary mania for forming collections.

PASSAGE 2

Extract 1 from Autobiography

I had many friends amongst the schoolboys, whom I loved dearly, and I think that my disposition was then very affectionate. Some of these boys were rather clever, but I may add on the principle of 'noscitur a scio' ('by his friends he is known') that not one of them ever became in the least distinguished.

5 With respect to science, I continued collecting minerals with much zeal, but quite unscientifically: all that I cared for was a new *named* mineral, and I hardly attempted to classify them. I must have observed insects with some little care, for when at ten years old (1819) I went for three weeks to Plas Edwards (Barmouth) on the sea coast in Wales, I was very much interested and surprised at seeing a
10 large black and scarlet hemipterous insect, many moths (zygaena) and a cicindela, which are not found in Shropshire. I almost made up my mind to begin collecting all the insects which I could find dead, for on consulting my sister,

20

I concluded that it was not right to kill insects for the sake of making a collection. From reading White's *Selbourne* I took much pleasure in watching the habits of
15 birds, and even made notes on the subject. In my simplicity I remember wondering why every gentleman did not become an ornithologist.

Extract 2 from Autobiography

But no pursuit at Cambridge (1828) was followed with nearly so much eagerness or gave me so much pleasure as collecting beetles. It was the mere passion for collecting, for I did not dissect them and rarely compared their external
20 characters with published descriptions, but got them named anyhow. I will give proof of my zeal: one day, on tearing off some old bark, I saw two rare beetles and seized one in each hand: then I saw a third and new kind, which I could not bear to lose, so that I popped the one which I held in my right hand into my mouth. Alas, it ejected some intensely acrid fluid, which burnt my tongue so that
25 I was forced to spit the beetle out, which was lost as well as the third one.

Extract 3 from Journal (1832)

During my stay at Brazil I made a large collection of insects . . . I was much surprised at the habits of *Papilio feronia*. This butterfly is not uncommon and generally frequents the orange-groves. Although a high flier, yet it very frequently alights on the trunks of trees. On these occasions its head is invariably
30 placed downwards; and its wings are expanded in a horizontal plane, instead of being folded vertically, as is commonly the case. This is the only butterfly which I have ever seen that uses its legs for running. Not being aware of this fact, the insect, more than once, as I cautiously approached with my forceps, shuffled on one side just as the instrument was on the point of closing and thus escaped. But
35 a far more singular fact is the power which this species possesses of making a noise. Several times when a pair, probably male and female, were chasing each other in an irregular course, they passed within a few yards of me; and I distinctly hear a clicking noise, similar to that produced by a toothed wheel passing under a spring catch. The noise was continued at short intervals, and could be
40 distinguished at about twenty yards' distance: I am certain there is no error in the observation.

Questions on Passage 1

Marks

(a) State **two** things you can deduce about the natural historian, Gilbert White, from the reference to him in lines 1 – 3.   2

(b) Explain what is meant in lines 36 – 37 by the expression
". . . all the freshness of unalloyed ignorance."   2

21

(c) What general point is being made in the opening paragraph?   **1**

(d) Demonstrate that the opening sentence of paragraph two (lines 17 – 18) acts as a linking device in the argument.   **2**

(e) Read the second paragraph (lines 17 – 31) carefully.

    (i) What reason does the author give for considering Victorian naturalists' explanations of their popularity to be unconvincing and implausible?   **4**

    (ii) What alternative explanation does the author offer?   **2**

(f) Explain briefly the point being illustrated by the author's reference to Queen Victoria.   **1**

(g) Why, according to the author in the last paragraph (lines 42 – 56) did natural history appeal to well-to-do Victorians as a means of filling their leisure hours?   **1**

(h) Basing your answers on lines 49 – 56 explain in your own words three ways in which natural history satisfied Victorian attitudes to and outlook on life.   **3**

(i) What effect does the writer obtain by the repetition of "every" in paragraph one (lines 1 – 16)?   **1**

(j) Comment on the effectiveness of any **two** examples of the author's word choice in the second sentence of paragraph one from "it was impossible to visit the seaside . . ." to ". . . prodding at sea-anemones."   **2**

                                               (21)

Questions on Passage 2

(k) What do we learn of Darwin's character from his opening remarks?   **2**

(l) What do we learn about Darwin's sister from the second paragraph?   **2**

(m) The three extracts show stages in Darwin's development as a scientist.

    (i) How does the first extract show both his developing interest and youthfulness?   **2**

    (ii) To what extent has he advanced in the second extract and to what extent not?   **2**

    (iii) How do you realise from the last extract that he is a mature scientist?   **2**

                                               (10)

Questions on Both Passages

Marks

(n) How does the last sentence of Passage 1 tie in with Darwin's own account of his developing interest?   **2**

(o) What is the attitude of the writer of Passage 1 to the Victorian passion for natural history?
What tone does she use?
Quote a sentence or phrase to support this.   **3**

(p) What is Darwin's attitude to natural history?
Quote a phrase to support your view.   **2**

(q) What is the difference in the standpoint of the two writers?   **2**
(9)
Total marks (40)

QUESTION PAPER E

Refer to page 2 for Instructions to Candidates

The first passage is adapted from an article in *BBC Wildlife* magazine, in which Tess Lemmon looks at how we use images of animals to say something about ourselves. The second passage is an extract from *King Solomon's Ring* by Konrad Lorenz from the chapter entitled *Laughing at Animals*.

PASSAGE 1

The Menagerie of the Mind

I spend a lot of time at zoos, and sometimes will stand for hours in front of one cage. But what I am watching is the people, the zoo visitors, the pigs-in-the-middle in a game where the "pro-zoo scientific lot" and the "anti-zoo emotional lot" throw their mud-bespattered missiles at each other.

5　It doesn't take many hours of lurking at the cage side to experience at first-hand the truth of an English Tourist Board zoo-visitor survey which found that "7 per cent of the visitors went to learn something about animals and birds; 64 per cent went to have a day out". Tempting though it is to get self-righteously angry at visitors responding to the animals with banal comments, inane chatter and
10　predictable jokes, it's interesting to ask what is behind those responses, and try to glimpse something about our knowledge of and interest in animals.

Loss of contact with the natural world is much discussed and mourned, and the plastic packages of pink protein in supermarket freezers show how out of touch we are. Yet we are surrounded by animals and their representations.

15　Take the tiger. It's on your breakfast table (They're G-r-r-eat!) and in the petrol tank of your car. It's made into arty posters and greetings cards. It's on T-shirts and logos. Tigger bounds through everybody's childhood. There is even Tiger cheese.

Animals are everywhere — hawks, doves, bears and eagles, lions and bulldogs,
20　wolves in sheep's clothing, penguins, puffins . . . These everyday images are as much cultural stereotypes as are the typical feminine female, the macho male, the ideal husband. In fact they say more about *people* than animals. The ESSO tiger tells us little about tigers, but much more about our concepts of freedom, beauty, invincibility.

25　Watching people watching animals is indeed fascinating. My impression is that many zoo visitors arrive and leave with their assumptions intact, seeing what they

'know' and isolating physical features and reputations seen somewhere recently. Responses have been decided long before the actual thing has been encountered. People express what their *idea* of the animal is, and children pick up appropriate
30 responses from parents. This is well illustrated with the reptiles; "Shall we go and see the s-s-snakes?" People enjoy squirming, and they gear themselves up to it. Men show off machismo, women their sensitivity by giggling and looking away.

Given that most people *are* out of touch with the natural world, it is not surprising that animals are related to in terms of human experience as well as
35 cultural stereotype. There are no other reference points. Mothers encourage children to say hello, wave goodbye; the tiger's flicking tail is a sign of friendship, the seal flaps its flipper in greeting, the bears are "looking at you".

The onus is on the zoos. They can keep animals in ways which inspire respect and interest in them for their own sakes, or they can reinforce the myths — for
40 instance by housing all the 'nasties' (reptiles and insects) together, or by encouraging the presentation of living animals as toys in children's zoos.

That the visitor has the capacity for involvement and enthusiasm shows itself when animals behave in ways which draw people in, making them forget their anthropocentricism. Then instead of chatter there is golden silence. People stand
45 in rapt concentration as otters play, as polar bears chase each other in the water, as a tiger stalks sparrows. Some feeding times have the same effect, with faces focused on animals *doing* something.

Even a simple notice can help. One near the monkeys at Twycross Zoo reads; "No, they are not picking fleas." One in the old aquarium at Bristol Zoo had
50 more impact than any other I saw. It explained that the mirror carp was rescued from a pond where the M32 was being built. This piece of information was being lapped up and passed on enthusiastically. It linked what was being seen with something in the everyday lives of the spectators.

In many cases the "pro-zoo" and "anti-zoo" lots are arguing for the same thing;
55 that we respect animals, understand how they live and stop destroying them in their homes. But as arguments how best to achieve this continue, zoo visitors see tigers as "disdainful", "fierce" and "vicious"; and jokes range from beautiful rugs to overgrown pussycats.

PASSAGE 2

It is seldom that I laugh at animals, and when I do, I usually find out afterwards that it was at myself, at the human being whom the animal has portrayed in more or less pitiless caricature, that I have laughed. We stand before the monkey house and laugh, but we do not laugh at the sight of a caterpillar or a snail, and when
5 the courtship antics of a lusty greylag gander are so incredibly funny, it is only our human youth behaves in a very similar fashion.

25

The initiated observer seldom laughs at the bizarre in animals. It often annoys me
when visitors at a Zoo or Aquarium laugh at an animal that, in the course of its
10 evolutionary adaptation, has developed a body form which deviates from the
usual. The public is then deriding things which, to me, are holy; the riddles of the
Genesis, the Creation and the Creator. The grotesque forms of the chameleon, a
puffer or an anteater awake in me feelings of awed wonder, but not of
amusement.

15 Of course I have laughed at the unexpected drollness, although such amusement
is in itself not less stupid than that of the public that annoys me. When the queer
land-climbing fish *Periophthalmus* was first sent to me and I saw how one of these
creatures leaped, not out of the water basin, but on to its edge, and, raising its
head with its puglike face towards me sat there perched, staring at me with its
20 goggling, piercing eyes, then I laughed heartily. Can you imagine what it is like
when a fish, a real and unmistakable vertebrate fish, first of all sits on a perch,
like a canary, then turns its head towards you like a higher terrestrial animal, like
anything but a fish, and then, to crown all, fixes you with a binocular stare? This
same stare gives the owl its characteristic and proverbially wise expression,
25 because, even in a bird, the two-eyed gaze is unexpected. But here too the
humour lies more in the caricature of the human, than in the actual drollness of
the animal.

In the study of the behaviour of the higher animals, very funny situations are apt
to rise, but it is inevitably the observer, and not the animals, that plays the
30 comical part. The comparative ethologist's method in dealing with the most
intelligent birds and mammals often necessitates a complete neglect of the dignity
usually to be expected of a scientist. Indeed, the uninitiated, watching the student
of behaviour in operation, often cannot be blamed for thinking that there is
madness in his method. It is only my reputation for harmlessness, shared with the
35 other village idiot, which has saved me from the mental home.

Questions on Passage 1

Marks

(a) Show how the context helps you to arrive at the meaning of
"stereotypes" (line 21).   2

(b) What contribution does the word "indeed" make to the meaning of the
sentence in line 25?   1

(c) "Tempting though it is . . . interest in animals." (lines 8 – 11)
What do these lines reveal about the writer's attitude to zoo visitors?   2

(d) Find **three** pieces of evidence from lines 25 – 37 which the author uses to
support the view that people are not humbled by their experience of
visiting zoos. (Remember to use your own words.)   3

26

(e) (i) "The onus is on the zoos." (line 38)
    What responsibility, according to the author, do zoos have?   1

(ii) Give one way in which the zoos, according to the author, "reinforce the myths".   1

(f) Read lines 42 – 47. The author claims that the zoo visitors can have a genuine interest in animals. What evidence does the author present in these lines to support this claim?   1

(g) (i) Explain fully the thinking behind the notice at Twycross Zoo, "No, they are not picking fleas". (line 49)   2

(ii) Discuss the significance of the notice about the mirror carp (line 50) in the author's argument.   2

(h) "But what I am watching . . . missiles at each other. (lines 2 – 4)
    Comment on the effectiveness of one example of word choice in this sentence.   2

(i) "Yet we are surrounded by animals and their representations."
    Explain how this sentence acts as a link between paragraphs 3 and 4.   2

(j) Comment on the use of the semi-colon in line 36.   1
    (20)

Questions on Passage 2

(k) (i) People often think they are laughing at animals. What does the author claim they are really laughing at?   2

(ii) What do the references to the caterpillar and the greylag goose add to his argument?   2

(l) (i) What kind of animals does Lorenz feel should never be laughed at?   2

(ii) Why does he feel this way about them?   2

(m) The example of the *Periophthalmus* relates to both his previous points.

(i) How does it relate to the point he is making in paragraph 1?   2

(ii) How does it relate to the point he is making in paragraph 2?   2
    (12)

Questions on Both Passages

(n) In paragraph 4 of Passage 2 the writer comments on the comic nature of the person observing animals.

Quote a sentence from Passage 1 which makes a similar point.　　1

(o) What **two** reasons for observing animals are given in paragraph 2 of Passage 1?

Which of these reasons do you think applies to the Konrad Lorenz extract?　3

(p) Both of the writers try to lighten their subject matter with humour. Give an example of humour from each passage and explain the nature of the humour.　　4

(8)

Total marks **(40)**

QUESTION PAPER F

Refer to page 2 for Instructions to Candidates

The first passage has been taken from R.W. Reid's book *Tongues of Conscience*, an interesting and lively account of the development of science and technology over the past 75 years. The author has previously introduced the reader to the Theory of Relativity and has described how it was verified by British scientists in 1919. He is now trying to account for the rapid rise to public fame of its formulator, Albert Einstein. The second passage is from *Einstein for Beginners* by Joseph Schwartz and Michael MacGuiness, a Writers and Readers Documentary Comic Book.

PASSAGE 1

Among scientists Einstein's genius had been both recognized and acknowledged for 14 years but it was only now that the public at large became aware of him. It is difficult to analyse the source from which the world-fame of Einstein sprang so suddenly. The public was undoubtedly well aware that there were strange
5 happenings in the traditionally unshakeable temples of science; in Britain, for example, some of its most honoured scientists had had to acknowledge that the stature of its greatest scientific genius, Newton, had been bent in places by a German-Swiss clerk. Moreover the popular press found copy in Einstein and in the apparently far-reaching consequences of his theories. Newspaper
10 photographers discovered a highly photogenic and, for a time at least, tolerant subject: his was a face of character: drooping, kindly eyes and wrinkles of humour surrounded by a leonine mane of hair. The habits of the man were a little irregular; already some of the characteristics expected of the absent-minded professor were beginning to show: he lived a simple life uncluttered by
15 possessions and any of the outward trappings of success; when there was no need to be careful he was careless about his dress: sometimes he wore no socks.

All these qualities, combined with the publicised qualities of the man, kindliness, gentleness and warmth, would still not have been sufficient to turn Einstein into the international figure he was to become. The missing ingredient in this recipe
20 for public fame was the apparently incomprehensible nature of Einstein's work. For a few years after the publication of the general theory of relativity only a limited number of scientists familiarised themselves with it in detail. Its abstruse nature became legend and absurd stories sprang up around its esoteric significance. It was even rumoured that there were few men in the world who
25 were capable of understanding the theory. One story had it that a newspaper

29

reporter had approached Sir Arthur Eddington and said that he had heard that there were only three people who were truly able to understand Einstein's work. "Really?" was supposed to have been Eddington's reply. "And who's the third?" Popularisations of relativity theory appeared in the newspapers and magazines of
30 a world which, after four years of war, was delighted to read something other than stories of trenches, wounded, rehabilitation or peace conferences. In most cases the popularisers failed to remind their readers that if the author of relativity theory had been best able to express his work in non-mathematical language then he would probably have done so. The satisfactory outcome of this great burst
35 of popularisation was that a part of physics, in the name of Einstein and in the name of 'Relativity', entered common culture. The tousled-haired man became the subject of cartoons, the butt of jokes ("Tell me Dr. Einstein, what time does this station stop at the next train?"); and because of his singular casual Bohemian appearance he became the epitome of the scientist. The unsatisfactory outcome
40 of it all was that Einstein was assumed to have a deeper insight than others into subjects of which he claimed no special knowledge. Vaguely it was known that his work had revolutionised scientists' concepts of space and time, and therefore it was believed that in some way Einstein was dabbling with space and time and perhaps even dabbling with things quite near to God. Whatever the nature
45 of the reasons the result was surprising: Einstein was the first scientist to become a world figure in his lifetime.

PASSAGE 2

Extract 1

The speed of waves depended only on the medium and not on the source. For example, according to wave theory, sound from a passing train covers the distance to the observer in the same time no matter how fast the train is moving. And Maxwell's equations predicted the same thing for light. The observer on
5 the ground should always see the light leaving Albert's face at the same speed no matter how fast Albert was moving.

But if the observer on the ground were to see the same speed for the light leaving Albert's face no matter how fast Albert was moving, then Albert should be able to catch up to the light leaving his face and his image should disappear.

10 But if his image shouldn't disappear then light leaving his face should travel towards a mirror normally. But then the observer on the ground should see the light travelling towards the mirror at twice its normal speed. But if the observer on the ground . . . Oy veh!

Albert began to see if there
were any way for the speed
of light to be the SAME for BOTH
the moving and ground observers!

Extract 2

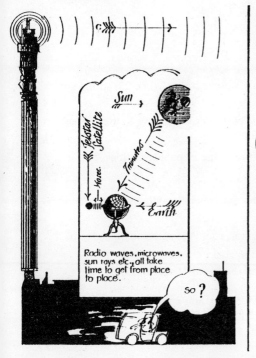

So Albert made an inference. Based on the experience with electricity as summarised by Maxwell and verified by Hertz, Albert proposed that there are no instantaneous interactions at all in nature.

Here is the simple **physical** meaning of Albert's 2nd postulate:

Every interaction takes time to get from one place to the next.

And if there are no instantaneous interactions in nature then there must be a maximum possible speed of interaction.

This is so important we will repeat it.: If there are no instantaneous interactions in nature then there must be a maximum possible speed of interaction.

Questions on Passage 1

Marks

(a) What points does the author wish to make about science when he uses the words "unshakeable" and "temples" (line 5)?　　　　2

(b) What is the effect on meaning of the author's use of:
　(i) "for a time at least" (line 10)
　(ii) "apparently" (line 20)?　　　　2

(c) Examine the context (lines 34 – 39) of the expression
　　　"common culture."
Say what this expression means and explain how the CONTEXT helped
you arrive at the meaning.　　　　2

(d) What one "strange happening" (lines 4 – 5) in science is referred to by the author?   1

(e) Why according to the information contained in lines 8 – 16, did the press become interested

    (i) in Einstein's theories, and   1

    (ii) in the man himself?   3

(f) Examine carefully lines 17 – 34.

    (i) Why, according to the author, did "absurd stories" (line 23) spring up about Einstein's theory?   2

    (ii) What made the public at that time particularly receptive to the various popularisations of Einstein's work?   1

    (iii) Why, according to the author, did these popularisations fail to elucidate Einstein's theory?   1

(g) In lines 34 – 46 the author considers the consequences of the popularisation process.

    (i) In what ways, according to the author, could the outcome be said to be satisfactory?   2

    (ii) What, according to the author, was the unsatisfactory outcome?   2

(h) The author introduces into the second paragraph an anecdote about Sir Arthur Eddington (lines 25 – 28) and a joke concerning Einstein (lines 37 – 38). Choose one OR the other and say for what purpose the author includes it?   1

(i) Demonstrate that the sentence beginning "All these qualities . . ." (line 17) performs an important linking function between the two paragraphs of the passage.   2

                                                                                 (22)

Questions on Passage 2

(j) Which theory in lines 1 – 6 gave rise to the joke in Passage 1 "Tell me Dr. Einstein, what time does this station stop at the next train?"   2

(k) How does the context help you to arrive at the meaning of "instantaneous" in the second section of the cartoon?   2

Marks

(l) (i) Why is the first word on the second section of the cartoon "So"? **2**

    (ii) What phrase could have been used instead? **1**

(m) (i) Explain which deduction is being illustrated by the man on horseback? **2**

    (ii) How is this further developed in the third drawing? **1**

(10)

Questions on Both Passages

(n) Why do you think the first passage refers to Einstein throughout as "Einstein" or "Dr. Einstein", while the second one refers to him as Albert? **2**

(o) Both passages are trying to make a man who developed a very difficult theory more accessible to ordinary people/non-physicists. Explain how each of them tries to do this and say which you find most effective. **6**

(8)

Total marks (40)

QUESTION PAPER G

Refer to page 2 for Instructions to Candidates

TO THE SOUND OF A DIFFERENT DRUM

Tom Morton, on the eve of a Runrig concert in Edinburgh, assesses the band's unique place in the rock pantheon.

Green's Playhouse had just metamorphosed, courtesy of new seats and a meagre lick of paint, into the Apollo. The year was 1973, and the broadsheet *Evening Citizen* was still being sold on the streets of Glasgow, that night with a free glossy poster. Inside, the Apollo smelled the way it always would over the following 13
5 years of my near-religious attendance there; overlying the eternal clammy fustiness of the place were the odours of sweat, perfume, toilets, aftershave and that fairground aroma of onions, hamburgers and bad coffee.

Billy Preston was the support act, but when the main attraction arrived on that unbelievably high stage he was still there, huddled in a corner with his Hammond
10 organ. The upper circle began to bounce alarmingly to the stamping of several hundred feet as Keith windmilled into his guitar and *Brown Sugar* introduced me to live rock music. The Rolling Stones came to Glasgow and messed up both my hearing and my critical sensibilities. I was deaf for four days afterwards, and inoculated against any other band's claims to divinity for more than a decade.

15 By the 1980s, I had been forced by penury into rock journalism. By then the Glasgow music scene was about style, hipness, millions in mythical record company advances, whether or not Wet Wet Wet would sign for Liverpool, if Kane Brothers calling themselves Hue and Cry was really such a good idea, which night club would let hacks in for free and in front of the queue. Cynicism
20 was de rigueur, black soul was the overriding influence and a band called Runrig were a bunch of ageing teuchters with dubious moustaches, dreadful jackets and worse haircuts. Their music? No-one had actually listened to it, although didn't they cover *Loch Lomond* when they weren't heederum-hoderumming in some dead language nobody understood and fewer spoke?

25 In 1992 things are different. The recession has bitten deep into pop profitability. Scotland is no longer the destination for droves of deaf record company executives. Even the Scottish bands who came out of the mid-eighties Glasgow scene are finding things more of a struggle. Deacon Blue, Hue and Cry, Wet Wet Wet — no longer hip, or happening, their hold on the transient glories of popdom
30 has weakened or slipped entirely. I am into night feeding, not night clubbing.

In 1991, the much-maligned Runrig are on top. Built to last, their continual refinement of rock and folk styles into a streamlined, anthemesque form of their

34

own has gripped vast numbers of Scots, from toddlers to grannies. They are not,
like the rapidly wrinkling Stones, still raw, petulant, nasty and dangerous,
35 because they never were in the first place. But exciting they are. And important.

It was 1984 when I first saw Runrig, playing in a drizzle-drenched Queen's Park
at Glasgow Fair. I'd been nagged to go and see what was even then something of
a phenomenon. It was very strange. As the moment came for the band to go on
stage, hundreds of shadowy figures converged on the venerable bandstand in
40 the dampness and the gloom. They were like no other rock crowds I'd seen. All
ages, all dress styles were represented, from families in matching Icelandic
sweaters and umbrellas to unhealthy-looking Goths with black lipstick dribbling
down their chins. Hipness was irrelevant.

Then Runrig played, and it was like nothing I'd ever heard. Great slabs of
45 Seventies rock imbued with Celtic fire and bounce. Lyrics which, even in English,
seemed to touch a nerve in the bosom of even the most cynical Caledonian. And
Donnie Munro's voice, that pure Hebridean tremolo so bizarre, yet so powerful
in a context of distorted guitar and rock rhythms.

True, they looked very odd, half hippy throwbacks at a time when long hair was
50 seriously questionable, half-grown-up teachers playing at rock body shapes. But
songs like *Dance Called America* and *Skye* gripped and would not let go. It was a
mixture of emotion, poetic content and sheer noise, calculated to appeal to those
consciously or subconsciously dispossessed of their nationhood, Gaelic speakers
or not.

55 For Gaels, Runrig obviously represented much more. Back then, before the
Government's £9-million Gaelic media funding, before Gaelic was remotely cool,
when the language was still deciding whether to die on its feet or not, Runrig
were the only indigenous heroes that younger Gaels had. And they were making
the most of them.

60 It was nothing like as consuming an experience as that long-ago Stones gig. But in
its own way, Runrig at Queen's Park changed my perceptions of Gaeldom, and of
rock's possibilities. Here was a band whose essential power came not from
America's black culture but from their own heartland, from Skye and the
Gaidhealtacht. Here was rock music which was uplifting, emotional, steeped in
65 history; highly political, but specifically so, dealing with issues like land
ownership which were rooted in the band's own cultural experience. And not
balancing on that tightrope of violence and danger which had always hallmarked
great rock to me; these were rebels with a very well worked out cause indeed.

The songs of Calum and Rory Macdonald are imbued with the sadness of the
70 Gaels' great losses, the spiritual succour and guilt which gives those physical
elements like the land, the community and the family both context and content,
and a deep-rooted socialism. They are not a Nationalist band.

35

Not Nationalist, but about nationhood. When Donnie sings Calum's lyrics about *The Edge of the World* or about coming home, the appeal of Runrig's
75 perspective, even to Scots who thing Gaelic is a herb added to butter in wine bars, is overwhelming. It's a way of seeing Scotland, not through the dirt-smeared windows of the cities, but from the north, from mountains and the sea and the battlefields and the generations of those who worked the land; out of the heritage all of us wish we had comes the music which offers identity.

80 Place is important to Runrig. For them, performing on Edinburgh Castle esplanade is not just about giving east of Scotland fans a chance to see them. It's about playing in the very centre of Scottish nationhood. They won't admit it, but there is an element of reclamation involved. The strong-hold of the Scottish military will fall to a bunch of renegade-but-polite Gaels singing about tearing
85 down landlords' fences, about the destruction of the clans, about mountains and rivers and the sea and the spirit of the past.

Songs like *Siol Ghoraidh*, about the battles fought by former generations; and *Flower of the West*, using Uist's physical glories as symbols of religious insight. The castle will still be standing after these concerts, but for those who were there,
90 it will speak in the future not of military glory but of musical celebration, of a spiritual, emotional and very noisy unity which will make the Tattoo seem tame, and leave Mons Meg gaping in blank astonishment.

The Scotsman Weekend, 24th August, 1991.

QUESTIONS

Marks

1. Look at the first paragraph. How does the writer recreate the atmosphere of the "Apollo" between 1973 and 1986?   4

2. ". . . inoculated against any other bands' claims to divinity."
   What is implied by this image of the writer's experience?   2

3. Look at lines 15 – 24. How did Runrig fit into the pop scene of the 1980s?   4

4. What are the **two** causes of change in the pop scene since the 1980s?   2

5. "I am into night feeding, not night clubbing."
   Explain what you think the writer means by this.   1

6. What was unusual about the crowds at the first Runrig concert the writer attended?   2

7. Look at lines 44 – 48. Define the different elements which, according to the writer, make up the music of Runrig.   4

36

8. (i) Which particular group in Scotland did they seem to represent?   **1**

  (ii) What circumstances encouraged this feeling?   **3**

9. "Rebelliousness" is often associated with rock groups.
What, according to the writer, is the difference between the rebelliousness
of other rock groups and Runrig?   **4**

10. What distinction does the writer try to make between "Nationalist" and
"nationhood" (line 73)   **2**

11. Lines 75 – 76. Explain fully the significance of the joke.   **3**

12. ". . . not just about giving east of Scotland fans a chance to see them"
What is the real significance of the Runrig's performance on Edinburgh
Castle esplanade, according to the writer?   **2**

13. The Rolling Stones are mentioned three times, (lines 12, 34, 60).
Explain the relevance of each reference to the different stages of the
writer's argument.   **6**

Total marks (40)

QUESTION PAPER H

Refer to page 2 for Instructions to Candidates

The first passage is an extract from an article in the *New Internationalist* by Martin Mittelstaedt called *Crime Wave*. The second is an extract from *Life After Life* by Tony Parker in which a prisoner serving a life sentence describes some of his experiences.

PASSAGE 1

Thirty-one people are murdered in New York on a typical week, a death toll that rivals fatalities in most other countries only when there are great calamities, such as civil war or natural disasters. There were 1,598 murders in 1986, a tally well beyond anything recorded in Europe or in most Third World countries.

5   The soaring crime rate has produced a culture of fear and paranoia in New York that is quite unlike most major cities outside the U.S. Fear of crime has shaped life in New York, dictating where people live and whether they feel safe enough to walk to the corner store. New York's preoccupation with personal security has created a whole new industry catering to citizens fearful of the city's huge

10 criminal underclass. The industry offers everything from security guards to razor wire which can be spread judiciously around vulnerable locations on apartment or office buildings to deter intruders.

Rich New Yorkers live in buildings with around-the-clock guards and barred windows — an expensive form of house arrest. Everyone who visits or lives in the

15 city is affected by the grim reality of crime. Tourists are cautioned to avoid parks after dark and to lock car doors when travelling in dangerous areas. Even U.N. diplomats are warned about crime. An official publication titled *New York, Your Host* lists nine points to help newcomers from becoming unwitting victims.

I felt this crime paranoia my first day in New York after I'd accidentally locked

20 myself out of my apartment building. I'd just arrived from Toronto to begin a reporting assignment and thought getting back inside would be easy.

But as I waited on the steps, my neighbours, who had not seen me before, slammed the self-locking door in my face or physically blocked me from entering. They were afraid to allow me into the building. Protests that I actually lived there

25 were brushed aside.

38

The main method used to deter crime is the usual one — the threat of prison. In
the U.S. as a whole, three out of every 100 adult males were either incarcerated
or under some form of correction supervision at the end of 1985. Nearly three
million men and women are in prison or on probation, a disproportionate
30   number of them poor black and Hispanic.

Although the jails are brimming, crime statistics have not budged. There were
500 000 felonies (robberies, assaults, rapes and murders) reported to New York
City police last year, a figure that hasn't changed appreciably since 1983. Many
criminal activities are not reported, so it is likely the real tally is substantially
35   higher. Still, official numbers suggest a typical New Yorker is likely to be a victim
of serious crime about five times in a lifetime.

Both police and citizens are understandably jumpy. In fact the culture of crime
has exacerbated tensions between police and citizens so much that 5000
complaints about arbitrary, often brutal police conduct were sent to the Police
40   Review Board in 1986.

The recent case of a subway rider acquitted for shooting four black youths who
he feared were going to rob him demonstrates graphically the power of these
fears. The teenagers, one of whom was paralyzed in the shooting, said they were
begging. The man became a local hero and was even encouraged to run for
45   mayor.

The effect of this is to strip New York of its civility. Common decency has been
hijacked and trust between ordinary people undermined. The causes and
consequences of crime have become so confused that the underlying issue of the
polarization of power and opportunity in New York is lost in the mists of fear.

PASSAGE 2

It was an old con in prison first sussed me out. Some of those old men in there,
they'd spent nearly their whole lives in prison doing long sentences. They'd be
out for a few months, maybe a couple of years, then get caught and be back
inside. They'd have started their lives of crime when they were young, perhaps
5   in their twenties, and you'd meet them and go on meeting them, each different
prison you were sent to, when they were 40, 50, 60, doing maybe another ten
years. They were big men quite a few of them, I mean big in crime, household
names almost. Sort of professors in university. If you wanted to learn about crime
you would learn everything from them. If you wanted to learn how to survive in
10   prison that was another thing you could learn. They were men of standing, they
had brains.

My first six or seven years inside after my life sentence I was fighting for survival. Literally fighting, the same as I had done in approved school and detention centre. Keeping up the hard image, fighting with the other cons and then
15 fighting with the screws who came to sort it out.

What started me telling you this? Oh aye the old con. He was a man, then about 60 I suppose: he'd done a long, long time and he was still going to do a long time more. Years back he'd killed a policeman, and they don't like that; you'll do longer for killing a policeman than for anything else there is. I'd been down on
20 punishment for the tenth time or however many it was, and he took me aside one day and told me authority was beating me. I said to him; "That's just what they're not doing and I'm showing them they're not." "They are," he said, "they are; you'll never beat the prison system that way, it's too big, too powerful. They can go on doing it to you for as long as they want; and you let them go on doing it,
25 they will."

The way I was doing my sentence, he said to me, was the hardest way there was. And what was I doing it for? What was I trying to prove, that they weren't going to beat me? What I was proving was they were. And then he said, I remember his words exactly, he said; "You know Andy, going on behaving like you are, you're
30 giving yourself no sort of life, son, at all."

I burst out laughing. Doing a life sentence and being told I was doing no sort of life. I thought it was the funniest thing anyone'd ever said to me.

Only those words sank in they did. They stayed in my head, they made me think. We talked a few times more, and he said things like there was nothing to get out
35 of a life sentence except what you put into it. The options you had as to what you could put into it were strictly limited; but there were a few things you could do if you had a mind to. "Oh yes, such as what?" "Study." "Study. Me?" "Yes, study, you." I gave my usual response, a foul mouthed slagging-off. Then the next day he came round to it again. And the next.

© *Tony Parker 1990.*

Questions on Passage 1

Marks

(a) Show how the contexts help you to arrive at the meanings of "paranoia" (line 5) and "incarcerated" (line 27).   **4**

(b) Look at paragraph 1. How does the writer use figures to emphasize the point he is making about crime in New York?   **4**

40

(c) "house arrest": comment on the author's use of this expression in the light of his previous remarks.   2

(d) What does the writer's anecdote about himself (lines 19 – 25) contribute to his discussion?   2

(e) The writer is concerned about the social problems resulting from the general public's fears of violence. Look at lines 37 – 45 and explain two of the possible consequences of such fears.   2

(f) "Common decency has been hijacked." Comment on the effectiveness of this image.   2

(g) (i) In the last paragraph he suggests one of the causes of the violence. Explain in your own words what he thinks this might be.   2

   (ii) When he discussed the prisons earlier in the passage he gave information which could support his theory. Explain what it is.   2

(20)

Questions on Passage 2

(h) "professors in university". Do you consider this to be an appropriate image for the older prison inmate?   3

(i) What indications are there that this is more or less a literal transcript of the ex-prisoner's words?   2

(j) Explain what you think the older man meant by "authority was beating me".   2

(k) "literally" (line 13). How does the context help you to understand the meaning of this word?   2

(l) "Those words sank in, they did."
   (i) Which words is he referring to?   1
   (ii) Why do you think he found them so memorable?   2

(12)

Questions on Both Passages

Marks

(m) Each writer is concerned with crime but from a different position. Explain what the difference is.　　2

(n) Look at the lines 19 – 25 in passage 1 and lines 12 – 15 in passage 2.

　(i) Each writer is faced with problems because of crime. Explain the difference in the way they react.　　2

　(ii) Look at the language each uses to describe this experience. Explain which one you think expresses himself most vividly.　　2

(o) The first writer is a journalist; the second an ex-prisoner. Quote **one** expression from each which might have led you to realise this even if you had not been told.　　2

　　　　　　　　　　　　　　　　　　　　　　(8)

　　　　　　　　　　　　　　　　Total marks　(40)

APPENDIX 1

Guide to Answers on Interpretation

QUESTION PAPER A

Answers to Questions in Passage 1

Read the passage at least twice before you attempt to answer.

(a) This is a common type of question. The context is that part of the text which is close to the given phrase/word; either just **before** it or just **after**.

You must refer to an explanation, an example or even an opposite which will give a clue to the meaning being asked for.

Always give the meaning of the phrase/word first; then give the explanation.

Answer

"arrests of mortality" means ways of holding back the consequences of being human such as being subject to the passing of time and to death.   **1**

We realise this because there are two examples before it which illustrate the meaning — the leaves which are saved from the flood, and the prizes which are kept from the dark and still admired.   **1**

(2)

(b) A question like this calls upon your general knowledge. You must show you understand the reference in the passage by relating it to your wider knowledge and general reading.

Explain the **one** example you have chosen and refer to examples you know of. These can be general rather than specific.

Answer

"exposure": to reveal someone's treachery or dishonesty.   **1**

For example a spy.   **1**

(2)

Any other answer from below would be marked in the same way.

Confession: to admit a failing in the hope of being forgiven, e.g., a film star on his/her love life.

Apologia: to explain why something was done which might appear to be wrong but the writer wants us to understand, e.g., a politician's actions.

Revenge: to tell about an event in order to hurt someone who has done wrong to the writer, e.g., a rejected husband/lover.

(c) Here you are being asked to give meanings with perhaps an example from everyday life to help your explanation.

Be careful to pick up the emotional content of the phrases

Remember there are two parts to the quotation.

Answer

"one supressing an incident as too much to bear" means that a person will crush down or deliberately forget an occasion where he was embarrassed or humiliated, e.g. ran away from danger.   1

"another building it large around him" means another person will not only remember fully an occasion which showed him in a good light but may even add little details to enhance the original story, e.g. his answer may be reported as even wittier than it really was.   1

                                                                                    (2)

(d) Notice you are being asked to consider only the **first paragraph**. You must choose and not quote the whole paragraph.

Read both parts of the question: the answer to part (ii) gives the clue to the answer to (i).

You must use your own words.

Answer

(i) His reason is to express his joy in life   1
     and to hold on to/keep alive all he has felt in life.   1
                                                                                    (2)
(ii) The expression "but for me" indicates that this is **his** reason.   **(1)**

(e) This is a common type of question. You are looking at the structure of the passage and the position of the given sentence in that structure.

The sentence will have one part that refers to what has gone before and one part that refers to what follows.

Answer

"A wasting memory is not only a destroyer": the phrase "not only" picks up the reference to other destroyers   1
which have been referred to in the previous paragraph, erosion, etc. and the fear that there will be nothing left.   1

"it can deny one's very existence." He is going on to explain in the rest of this paragraph what he means by this   1
i.e., it can do more than destroy; it can make it seem as though we never lived at all.   1

                                                                                    (4)

44

(f)   An anecdote is a small story.

You must look at the general argument at this point.

You must decide how the story illustrates or highlights what he is saying.

Answer

> Laurie Lee has been discussing **truth**; whether accurate facts are necessary for a story to be true or whether the truth lies in getting the emotions and understanding of people right.   **1**
>
> The story illustrates the attitude of some people; the aunt clearly believes that because he got a fact wrong (the name of the bride) that even the description of his mother is wrong. Laurie Lee shows that this is illogical.   **1**
>
>   **(2)**

(g)   A very common kind of question. You are being asked to discuss an image.

This usually takes the form of either

> a **simile**; a direct comparison
> a **metaphor**; an indirect comparison.

You should pick out the relevant point in the comparison and show how it relates to the author's argument.

In this case note that you are being asked to discuss three references.

> **drift**   **salt-caked**   **mud-flat**

All three images are linked to the sea going out, like time moving on. You must comment on this and on the idea expressed through what he describes as being left behind.

Answer

> "drift" suggests something moving away so slowly that its disappearance is hardly noticed.   ½
>
> This expresses his fear that memories may fade away before we have realised that we are forgetting them.   ½
>
> "Salt-caked" suggests an unattractive and lifeless residue left after all that is pleasant has vanished.   ½
>
> Salt is seen here in its bitterness not as a preservative. Lee is suggesting that only the bitter remnants of the past will remain in our memories.   ½
>
> **"mud-flat"** is similar in concept to **"salt-caked"**. When the tide has gone out all that is left is lifeless and dull.   ½
>
> So if our memories vanish we have nothing pleasant to look back on.   ½
>
>   **(3)**

(h) A straightforward question which involves you in explaining lines 1 – 8.

Answer

Gandhi says he wants to tell us about his attempts to find out about the nature of human experience and what its purpose is   **1**
and, since his life has consisted entirely of his attempts to find out this information, describing them will involve telling the story of his life.   **1**

    (2)

(i) Another question that asks for an explanation of an image and asks you to discuss how it helps the author's argument. You must trace the whole argument about openness and secrecy.

Answer

A closet is somewhere hidden from sight.   **1**
Gandhi rejects this image of his attempts to find out the answers to life's questions; his life is open for everyone to look at and criticise.   **1**
He goes on to acknowledge that there are some attempts to discover the meaning of life which are bound to be secret because they are between a man and his conscience/God.   **1**
He admits that he is not describing these, but those matters he is going to discuss are spiritually just as important.   **1**

    (4)

(j) Another question about an image; this time one relating to methods of working.

There is a direct comparison between the way a scientist works to find out physical truths and the way Gandhi tries to work to find out moral truths.

Answer

A scientist carries out experiments carefully and thoughtfully but even he can only hope that his results have taken everything into account.   ½ ½ ½

Nonetheless he must trust that his answers are correct   ½
and base his ideas on them while keeping an open mind.   ½
So Gandhi claims he has taken all precautions to make sure   ½
his search for truth is carried out accurately and honestly   ½
but he knows there is an element of trust about accepting   ½
that his conclusions are correct.   ½

    (4)

(k) You are looking for the meaning of this word by considering the words around it.

Answer

"infallibility" means having no possibility of being wrong.   **1**

EITHER:
The word is linked to "finality" which suggests something about which there can be no question and therefore we assume the idea of perfection.

OR:
Gandhi has been stressing that he hopes he is absolutely correct and parallels this with infallibility, though he acknowledges that this is an impossible ideal.   **1**

(2)

Answers to Questions in Both Passages

(l) You have studied the two passages thoroughly now. The two writers have a quite different idea about **truth** and the purpose of telling the story of a man's life. You should have grasped the overall difference in their assumptions now.

Answer

(i) Laurie Lee means there is no such thing as **truth** in isolation from a context. He believes that even factual truth is doubtful.   **1**
and any other hope for accuracy will depend on the point of view, circumstances and emotional reactions of the narrator. Unlike Gandhi he cannot separate humanity from his perceptions.   **1**

(2)

(ii) Gandhi is thinking in terms of himself in relation to God and a discovery of moral truth.   **1**
He wants to find out the truth about himself in relation to God and thus free himself from worldly emotional problems.   **1**

(2)

(m) There are many observations that you might make about Laurie Lee. He is emotional, perceptive, romantic, dislikes statistics, nostalgic about his childhood, etc. Choose the one that is clearest to you, pick out the piece of evidence and explain it.

Answer

Laurie Lee is romantic.   **1**
The example of the Taj Mahal shows this   **1**
because he obviously thinks the spirit of the building is much more important than the facts about it.   **1**

(3)

47

(n) Although Gandhi does not tell us such obvious things about himself as Laurie Lee nonetheless his personality comes through. He is clearly moral, serious, philosophical, perhaps even a little inhuman.

Answer

Gandhi was very moral.   1
He tells us he is trying to "see God face to face"   1
which suggests he took life seriously and believed absolutely in God
and in doing the right thing.   1
                                                                              (3)

APPENDIX II

Guide to Answers on Interpretation

QUESTION PAPER B

Answers to Questions in Passage 1

Read the passage at least twice before you attempt to answer.

(a) You should have read the passage twice by now and realise that it covers the topic of CFCs in aerosols, and their effect on the Ozone layer. The little story is an example of our attitude towards them and the use we find for them. You must explain the general point the writer is making.

Answer

The story in paragraph one gives an example/illustrates the writer's argument.	1
She is showing how useful aerosols are.	1
They appear to have almost miraculous qualities and so we keep them ready all the time without thinking of the dangers.	1
	(3)

(b) This question involves another example but the point being made is different. Be careful not to repeat the ideas already expressed in the first answer.

Answer

This example suggests we use them often for vanity not usefulness even when they are probably not going to do much good. ("(in my case) . . . unmanageable")	1
OR	
We also use them excessively ("a good spray").	1
	(2)

(c) (i) Up to this stage in the extract, and even after it, the author has been discussing CFCs. Clearly this paragraph will stand out because it is in a different print and on an apparently different topic. There are no linking words. However, a reader might read it before reading the rest of the passage. You must ask yourself why the author decided to do this. It is common practice in newspaper/magazine articles.

Answer

This passage is giving factual information which forms a background to what appears to be gossip about using aerosols.	1
The **bold** print means that a reader may have read this before starting and will certainly be aware of this information as he reads the rest.	1
	(2)

(ii) You must look ahead and find the part where the author links together this information about Ozone and her comments on aerosols and CFCs.

Answer

"Scientists who began to blame CFCs for the hole received short shrift — at first." **(1)**

(d) This is a fairly easy example of this kind of question. You must look at the words around it to find the indications of its meaning. Look before and after it.

Answer

"potentially" means having the possible power to do something. **1**
We know this because after it we find the word lethal which suggests radiation can kill, but we know that it is being prevented at the moment by the Ozone layer therefore its power has not been seen yet. **1**
(2)

(e) Remember the normal uses of quotation marks/inverted commas: titles or quotations and decide which one applies here.
You may know that this is a quotation from an advertisement in which case the answer is easy but even if you don't you can use your common sense.

Answer

EITHER
This is a quotation from an advertisement for the AA and therefore it has inverted commas.
OR
This sounds like a phrase commonly applied to people who have all the answers so it is like a quotation and has inverted commas. **(1)**

(f) You must look at the style here and relate the style to the information being given. The information is just more examples of the uses of aerosols but the style reveals our attitudes.

Note: questions and answers. The questions are in the form of statements.

the colloquial "Just spray" "So give", etc.,
the sharp commands,
the short clauses,
flippant phrases "good squirts" "handy can".

Answer

The writer is suggesting that we use the cans frequently/rashly **1**
and without thought. **1**
The flippant vocabulary suggests we don't think, e.g., "So give" and "squirts" and "handy can". **1**
The short questions followed by short commands suggests the answer is simple and requires no thought; we can do it over and over again. **1**
(4)

(g) This is a fairly common image and you might think that it is therefore simple and clear or you may decide that it is rather weak for describing something so important. You must refer to the picture this image invokes in your answer.

Answer

EITHER

This image is effective because we can all imagine the thinness of a common coin   **1**

and realise how thin and fragile this layer must be.   **1**

OR

This image is rather weak since a coin is rather hard and we think of the very small, circular shape rather than the thickness   **1**

and this is not appropriate for a layer of gas which extends right round the world.   **1**

         (2)

(h) (i) The question requires you to show that you have understood the basic point about the importance of the Ozone layer. You **must** use your own words to explain either lines 34 – 37 or line 43.

Answer

The Ozone layer absorbs dangerous beams from the sun and prevents them doing harm to the earth.   **(1)**

(ii) You must look at the list of effects given in the last paragraph and select the one that you think is intended to catch the attention of the reader. The indication comes from "most obvious".

Answer

The most important effect in the eyes of the author is the causing of skin cancer.   **1**

EITHER

She uses the expression "most obvious" and "most likely".

OR

She writes two sentences about it, not just adding it to the list.   **1**

         (2)

Answers to Questions on Passage 2

(i) Here you are being asked to look at an image and a symbol. Your general knowledge should give you an idea of the crown of thorns linked to the suffering of Christ. Even if you did not remember this you must realise that it is a painful image.

Answer

The image suggests that though the sun is powerful and magnificent, it also represents suffering. It is as though its very splendour is a mockery bringing pain to itself as well as the world   **1**
just as the crown of thorns placed on Christ's head indicated suffering both for Himself and the world.   **1**

(2)

(j) In this question you must watch out for two traps. Firstly you must use your own words not just quote the appropriate passage. Secondly you must give four points each worth half a mark; this should have occurred to you as soon as you realised that there were more than two different points to be made.

Answer

Water that is not flowing loses its life.   ½

Things that are still developing suddenly go bad and collapse.   ½

Whatever the sun touches becomes contaminated and deadly poisonous.   ½

We are left to imagine what the insects do but clearly it is frightening.   ½

(2)

(k) This question requires you to study lines 20 – 28 and make deductions from it. The advantage is fairly clear but you must find out the disadvantage by looking at what Sunder wants and working out that they must be in the opposite situation.

Answer

They are on a fast-flowing river which will not die under the sun and will protect them in some ways,   **1**
but the disadvantage is that there is no cover near the river and they are exposed to the rays of the sun.   **1**

(2)

(l) In this question you look for a grammatical clue, i.e., the tense of the verb.

Answer

Covenant uses the form "It used to be . . ." and "if you saw it" which tells us that he has seen this place before   ½
in quite different circumstances from the other characters.   ½

(1)

(m) Both these words have a simple meaning so you must not just give that meaning. You are being asked to explain the added implication of the prefix on the first word which makes it unusual. Think of all the reasons for using a capital letter and see which one applies to the second word.

Answer

> The word re-make implies that the land has been reduced to the pre-creation state and must now be created again from the beginning.   1
> The word Land has a capital letter to imply that it is the title of the country not just any part of the earth.   1
>
> **(2)**

(n) You must look at the style here and consider figures of speech. You do not need to remember the terminology but you could answer more easily if you knew the word onomatopoeia for the first quotation; and the concept of metaphor for the second.

Answer

EITHER

The word winced imitates the anguished sound (onomatopoeia) that we imagine him making as he speaks.

OR

The writer speaks as though the dismay, which is an emotion, were actually a solid substance which could fill Linden's mouth and choke her.   **(1)**

Answers to Questions on Both Passages

You should by now be fairly familiar with both passages. Some of these questions may appear to go over ground already covered but be careful to use the material to answer **these** questions most of which require you to compare the passages.

(o) This question requires you to have made a general observation about the second passage and to relate that observation to a specific reference from the first passage.

Answer

> The first passage refers to "dramatic and irreversible changes in weather patterns."   1
> The second clearly indicates that the sun is behaving in an unnatural way, and dominating the world.   1
>
> **(2)**

53

(p) (i) You are being asked to look at subject matter and style and to show how the combination arouses emotions, in this case fear.

Answer

The alliteration and meaning of the words "lethal levels" emphasises the deadly quality of the radiation.　　　　1
The two comparisons to the size of the hole 'the size of the USA' and 'deep as Mount Everest' emphasise how massive it is, since they are our highest mountain and a very big continent.　　　　1

(2)

(ii) You are looking for the same kind of thing here.

Answer

The reference to the past beauty arouses pity and nostalgia.　　　　1
Anger is aroused by emotive words like 'glared' 'gleams of rage' 'grated'.　　　　1
The abrupt short sentences give a rather melodramatic sense of urgency to the passage.　　　　1
The dialogue gives a sense of characters in action, and their exchanges add to the sense of urgency.　　　　1

Any two (2)

(q) This question requires you to use your general knowledge gathered over years of studying language and to give simple qualities of the two types of literature (genres) which are found in the two examples.

Answer

I know the first passage is from a magazine because it has:
A personal anecdote from the writer.　　　　1
It gives examples from everyday experience.　　　　1
It refers to information gathered.　　　　1
It mixes fact and opinion, e.g., lines 28 – 35, etc.　　　　1

Any two　(2)

I know the second passage is from a novel because it has:
A narrative/story line, i.e., they get up, etc.　　　　1
Characters with personalities who are part of the story.　　　　1
There is dialogue on an equal basis (i.e., not interview).　　　　1
The characters are planning for the future.　　　　1
The "Sunbane" appears to be imaginary.　　　　1

Any two　(2)

GLOSSARY OF TERMS

Sentence Structure — Syntax

You should be able to recognize ordinary sentences and to comment on variations. It is variations from the normal that you are usually asked to comment on. You might, in comparing two passages, be asked to note for example that one passage uses very short simple sentences, another long complex ones. The technical names are not essential but they may help you.

Simple

Subject : Verb : Object : Extension of the Verb
John   hit   the ball   into the garden.

Variations on this might be interesting, e.g., the object put first : *Into the garden, the ball John hit.* This gives greater importance to the place. It also sounds like a mockery of poetic sentence forms.

A series of simple sentence structures might be worth comment: most mature writers vary their sentence patterns. The intended effect might be to give an impression of speed, or to imitate a child writing.

Compound

Two simple sentences linked into one sentence and given equal importance, usually joined by *and, but* or *or.*

John hit the ball into the garden but Mary threw the bat through the window.

A repetition of this pattern would require comment.
The writer may be piling up a series of examples with *ands*; He may be setting one idea against another with *buts*; He may be giving a series of alternatives with *ors.*

Complex

One sentence consisting of several clauses (sentence structures) linked together by conjunctions, e.g., although, because, so that, when, after, where, etc.

Because he was tired / the boy hit the ball so gently / that it rolled into the garden / where a dog (which had been sleeping) woke up / and barked / because it had got a fright.

This style allows writers to relate one idea closely to another. If overdone it confuses rather than clarifies.

In questions about meaning be sure to check the links carefully.

In questions about style don't hesitate to say if you found this style difficult and therefore unattractive. Refer to an example to illustrate your opinion.

Sentences without Verbs

You may be asked about these.
They are used most often in poetry.
They are used in passages relying on emotional response.
They are used to surprise.
They attract attention if they are short.
They eliminate unneeded words thereby keeping attention on only what is interesting.

TYPES OF SENTENCE

Statement

I did that.
This is the most common form and only rarely requires comment.

Command

Do that!
This gives an imperative note to a passage, suggests urgency, requires action from others.

Exclamation

Do that!
This will give a sense of astonishment, anger or urgency. You imagine that the words are shouted.

Question

Did you do that?
A question is always looking for an answer.
It suggests active interest on the part of the questioner, a hope of interest on the part of the reader/hearer.

Rhetorical Question

This is a literary/oratorical device.
It is a question that does not expect an answer.
What would you do if the world ended tomorrow?
The writer may answer the question himself.
He may leave you to assume the answer is so obvious that there is no point in further discussion.
He may wish the reader to go and ponder the issue raised.

TENSES

You will have studied tenses in some detail in foreign languages. You will instinctively use and recognize tenses in English. You may be asked about occasions when a writer has deliberately used a "wrong" tense in his writing.

You should be able to recognize **past, present** and **future**.

You may be asked to comment on variations from the normal.

The most common variation is the use of the **present** in a passage clearly about the **past** and written mostly in the **past**.

This can be used to give a sense of immediacy.
It makes the reader feel he is actually present at an event.

Remember the technical terms may help but are not essential.

PUNCTUATION

Punctuation guides you through a passage. You may be asked to comment on unusual or interesting punctuation.

Full stop

This should end a complete sentence.
If full stops are missing, a passage is difficult to follow.
This can give the impression of thinking aloud.
Stream of consciousness, etc.

If a full stop is put in where it should not be, it brings the reader up short.
It gives extra importance to a phrase, word, etc.
It separates ideas forcefully that might have been linked.

Colon

The colon separates two clauses/sentence structures that are of equal importance and related to each other.

Speech is silver: silence is golden.

It is used after a general statement before a list of examples:

There were many reasons for him to be happy: he had a beautiful home; he had two fine children; he was rich.

Semi-colon

The semi-colon separates clauses that form part of a list. As above.
It separates a statement from further explanation.

Comma

This cuts off one clause from another.
It separates lists of single words.
Its most interesting use is as **brackets**. This is for asides, small explanations. This can be informative, explanatory or humorous.

The placing of a comma can alter the emphasis placed on a word or phrase.

Brackets (Parenthesis)

These are for extra information which is clearly not part of the main statement.
They are used for the same purpose as commas but are more decisive.

Dashes

They are often used for the same purpose as brackets (parenthesis).

One dash may be used to indicate a pause in thinking or before speech.

Inverted commas : Quotation marks

These mark speech or titles.
They may be used to indicate that speech is imagined, e.g., in a well known phrase.
They might be used in mock titles.

Punctuation is not interesting in itself.

You must recognize the way it affects STYLE and MEANING.

DESCRIPTIVE LANGUAGE

Literal and Non-Literal

Writers use straightforward description which is literal. They also use figurative/ imaginative/non-literal language which relies on **images — sound — tone — comparison — word association**, etc.

You might be expected to comment on any of these features.

Literal. All words have a literal accepted meaning: we all know what is meant by a "book" or a "boat". But even these words have **non-literal** overtones which go beyond the simple meaning.

Is a "ship" more glamorous or just bigger than a "boat"? Given a capital letter, does "Book" mean the Bible and all that that implies?

The English language makes use of the **non-literal** meaning of words. The most obvious examples are **figures of speech**. The technical terms will help you but you should be sensitive to all non-literal use of language.

FIGURES OF SPEECH

Metaphor

A metaphor implies a comparison between one thing and another. It can be direct:

That man is a shark.

Or be suggested by the use of words from one context placed in another context:

His anger burned itself out.

When asked to comment on a metaphor you should pick out the quality of the implied comparison and show how it applies to the thing being described, e.g.

Just as a shark has a reputation for viciousness and greed / so this man grasped everything in his path without thought for others.

e.g.

His anger was so great that after a time it faded away like a fire that blazes quickly and then dies down.

Simile

A simile makes a direct comparison. It compares two objects that are not the same:

She entered the room like a ship in full sail.

(Note; *One twin is like the other*, is not a simile, it is a literal comparison.)

Similes are easier to pick out than metaphors because they begin with *like* or *as*, but they are not as common in everyday speech.

You should comment on a simile in the same way as a metaphor, e.g.

Just as a ship with all its sails up looks large and imposing so the lady with her billowing dress and determined appearance looked important.

Symbol

A symbol is a word that carries significance because of the associations that have been built up around it:

a rose, the cross, harvest.

These words have been used so often in particular situations that it is impossible to ignore the extra meaning attached to them, e.g.

A *rose* suggests beauty that will fade.

Word association

Many words do not fall exactly into any of the above categories, but we all know the associations that they carry. *Bread*, *wine*, etc., are examples of words that can be interpreted literally or metaphorically.

SOUND

Alliteration

Alliteration uses the sound of repeated consonants to attract our attention: *The biggest balloon in Birmingham.* This can be used in a title to attract attention; it can be amusing to attract laughter; it can ridicule something ostentatious.

Onomatopoeia

This imitates the sound it is describing and adds an extra dimension: *Sizzling sausages squirted in the pan.* It helps to create realism; it makes the reader more sensuously aware; it reminds us that writing represents speech; it can be amusing.

Assonance

The repetition of vowel sounds but not consonants, e.g., shape and game and rate.

If the vowels are long as in the example it can slow down a passage. If they are short, e.g., hat, bad, jam, it makes a passage seem quick and sometimes amusing.

PLAYING WITH WORDS

Writers sometimes deliberately use language in a way that could be confusing; they do not always say exactly what they mean because they wish to add to the simple literal meaning.

Hyperbole

This is the use of intentional **exaggeration**.

There are thousands of people waiting.

This is used to stimulate action, to shock, etc. (If there were really thousands outside, of course the language would be literal and there would be no need for comment.)

Litotes

This is deliberate **understatement**. It is used to give a sarcastic effect, or as a joke.

During a heavy bombardment in a battle someone might say *It's a bit noisy here, don't you think.*

This can undermine the seriousness of a situation; It can suggest indifference on the part of the speaker. It can add a bitter tone to a passage.

Paradox

This is a **contradiction**. It usually consists of two statements which appear to be incompatible, e.g.

In the moment that she loved him most she hated him most deeply.

This contradiction should be impossible but we all understand the complexity of human emotions and know that we can feel apparently contradictory emotions at the same time.

Oxymoron

This is the technical term for a paradox which is expressed in two contradictory words, e.g. *bitter sweet; sweet sour* (smell).

Pun

This is the deliberate playing on the two possible meanings of one word. It takes advantage of the fact that English contains a lot of words which sound and are even spelled alike but which have different meanings. Usually this device is used for humour.

Ben Battle was a soldier bold . . .
A cannon ball shot off his legs
So he laid down his <u>arms</u>.

The effect here is intended to be humorous but it borders on the **macabre** (humour which is grim or cruel).

Juxtaposition

This is the deliberate placing of two words next to each other in such a way as to arouse surprise, amusement, interest, etc.   *She felt pleasantly angry.*

Context

This covers the surrounding area of text probably the rest of a paragraph.

Co-text

This covers words close to the word under discussion. It can be the same as **juxtaposition** or can cover words in the same sentence.

CLICHÉ

Any of the Figures of Speech shown above can become clichés if they are overused. Metaphors, similes, etc., which were original hundreds of years ago are no longer thought to be so.

She is as hard as nails.   She flew into a temper.   Silence is golden,   etc.

Some are used so often that they are hardly noticed in ordinary speech.

Using them too often might suggest that a writer is unimaginative.

It could, however, be a deliberate policy in a novelist to make a character who spoke entirely in clichés very boring, uninspired, i.e. his speech was appropriate to his character.

Sometimes a cliché in the midst of good original writing can attract attention to a universal truth.

REGISTER

This is the technical term for words, phrases and sentence structures which are associated with a particular group of writers or professionals. There are many registers which you will recognize, e.g., legal, medical, pop musical, etc.

Formal

This is the register that you are most often expected to use. It uses conventional sentence structure and straightforward vocabulary.

Jargon

This is the vocabulary associated with certain groups. It is a rather critical term; it implies that the vocabulary is being used deliberately to impress or even confuse.

A lawyer, doctor, etc., will naturally use the language of his profession. Imitating the jargon of a disc jockey, etc., might be amusing. Imitating the jargon of a politician might involve serious criticism as well as humour (**satire**).

The easiest aspect of register to recognize is vocabulary but try to recognize sentence structure too.

TONE

By the time you have studied all these aspects of a text you should have a good idea of the tone.

Tone is the emotional feel of a passage.

If it is **neutral** you are unlikely to be asked about it. This is the tone of **informative** passages with no point of view to put across.

Other tones to look for are: **amused, mocking, angry, indignant, enthusiastic, cynical, indifferent**, etc.

Sarcasm

This is one aspect of tone that you are often asked about. Sarcasm is where a writer says one thing but makes it clear that he means the opposite.

So we've lost the war. Well, that's wonderful!

We recognize sarcasm from the context. We know what the real response is likely to be and set these words against it.

Irony

This is linked to tone but also to the complete structure of a book, passage, etc. This is where a statement is made sincerely, perhaps by a character in a novel, but the reader's superior knowledge tells him that the statement is flawed.

Once I am king, I shall be happy!

We know that power rarely brings happiness.

ACKNOWLEDGMENTS

The author and publishers are grateful to the following for permission to use copyright material in this book.

Extract from *Save the Ozone Shield* by Judith Cook,
published in *She* Magazine

Extract from *The Wounded Land* by Stephen R. Donaldson *
reprinted by permission of Ballantine Books, a Division of Random House Inc.
* Copyright © 1980 by Stephen R. Donaldson

Extract from *To the Sound of a Different Drum* by Tom Morton
published by *The Scotsman Weekend* 24th August 1991.

Extract from *The Heyday of Natural History* by Lynn Barber
reprinted by permission of the Peters Fraser and Dunlop Group Ltd.

Extract from *The Menagerie of the Mind* by Tess Lemmon
first published in B.B.C. Wildlife Magazine

Extract from *King Solomon's Ring* by Conrad Lorenz
published by Methuen & Company

Extract from *Tongues of Conscience* by R.W. Reid
published by Constable Publishers

Extract from *Einstein for Beginners*
by Joseph Schwartz and Michael McGuiness

Extract from *Healey's Eye* by Denis Healey
reprinted by permission of Peters Fraser and Dunlop Group Ltd.

Extract from article by Peter Stalker
published by the *New Internationalist*, July 1988

Extract from an article by Martin Mittelstaedt
published by *New Internationalist*, December 1987

Extract from *Life After Life* by Tony Parker
reprinted by permission of Martin Secker and Wartburg Ltd.
© Tony Parker 1990

Printed by Martin's The Printers Ltd., Berwick upon Tweed